Co

3558 South Jefferson Avenue
St. Louis, MO 63118–3968
Manufactured in the United States of America

All Night, All Day

1. Day is dyin' in the west; angels watchin' over me, my Lord.
   Sleep, my child, and take your rest; angels watchin' over me.

Refrain

All night, all day, angels watchin' over me, my Lord.
All night, all day, angels watchin' over me.

2. Now I lay me down to sleep; angels watchin' over me, my Lord.
   Pray the Lord my soul to keep; angels watchin' over me.
   REFRAIN

3. Thy love stay with me through the night; angels watchin' over me, my Lord.
   And wake me with the morning light; angels watchin' over me.
   REFRAIN

Because of Love

Refrain

Oh, we've got hope for the future, assurance for eternity,
Life forever after in the fam'ly of God.

God gave us the gift of Jesus—
What a saving plan!
Jesus died, but three days later,
(*clap*)
He rose again!
He has made a home for us in heaven up above.
He did all of this because of love!
REFRAIN

Child of God

1. If anybody asks you who I am, who I am, who I am,
   If anybody asks you who I am,
   Say that I'm a child of God.

2. If anybody asks you how I am, how I am, how I am,
   If anybody asks you how I am,
   Say that I'm alive and free.

3. If anybody asks you what that means, what that means, what that means,
   If anybody asks you what that means,
   Say that I was born again.

4. If anybody asks you where I'm going, where I'm going, where I'm going,
   If anybody asks you where I'm going,
   Say that I am going to heaven.

5. If anybody asks you who's my Friend, who's my Friend, who's my Friend,
   If anybody asks you who's my Friend,
   Say that Jesus is His name.

For God So Loved the World

Refrain

For God so loved the world that He gave His only Son
That if we only believe in Him, we will have new life.

1. Jesus is our friend, His love will never end.
We know He loves us, really loves us;
We can trust in Him.
REFRAIN

2. Jesus gave His life so we will never die.
We know He cares for each of us,
He's with us all the time.

Refrain

For God so loved the world that He gave His only Son
That if we only believe in Him, we will have new life.
We will have new life.
We will have new life.

Go, My Children, with My Blessing

1. Go, My children, with My blessing, never alone;
Waking, sleeping, I am with you, you are My own.
In My love's baptismal river
I have made you Mine forever.
Go, My children, with My blessing, you are My own.

2. Go, My children, sins forgiven, at peace and pure.
Here you learned how much I love you, what I can cure.
Here you heard My dear Son's story,
Here you touched Him, saw His glory.
Go, My children, sins forgiven, at peace and pure.

3. Go, My children, fed and nourished, closer to Me;
Grow in love and love by serving, joyful and free.
Here My Spirit's power filled you,
Here His tender comfort stilled you.
Go, My children, fed and nourished, joyful and free.

4. I the Lord will bless and keep you and give you peace.
I the Lord will smile upon you and give you peace.
I the Lord will be your Father,
Savior, Comforter and Brother.
Go, My children, I will keep you and give you peace.

God Has Given Us His Word

1. God has given us His Word, it's written here!
   God has given us His Word, it's written here!
   God has given us His Word, it's written here!
   God has given us His Word, it's clear.

2. God has given us His Word, it's really true!
   God has given us His Word, it's really true!
   God has given us His Word, it's really true!
   God has given us His Word, it's true.

3. God has given us His Word, He's Jesus Christ!
   God has given us His Word, He's Jesus Christ!
   God has given us His Word, He's Jesus Christ!
   God has given us His Word to share.

God Is with Me

1. God is with me ev'rywhere I go
   Ev'ry day and night I always know
   He will never leave; He promises to be
   with me ev'rywhere I go.

2. When I am at church, at school, at home,
   I know I will never be alone.
   God will always be watching over me.
   I will never be alone.

God Loves Us

Refrain

We know that God loves us;
that's plain to see.
He's a Savior and a friend
for you and for me.

1. In His loving arms He holds us
ev'ry night and day.
When we're waking, when we're sleeping,
by us He will stay.
REFRAIN

2. With our friends and with our neighbors
we should always share,
always giving and forgiving,
showing them we care.
REFRAIN

3. Oh, what gifts and, oh, what blessings
God alone can give.
He has promised love and grace for
ev'ry day we live.
REFRAIN

God Made Adam

1. God made Adam, a very special man;
   God made Adam back when the world began.
   God made Adam, and then He made Eve.
   He gave them to each other—our first family.

2. God told Adam, "Don't eat from this one tree!"
   But Eve and Adam both wanted to be free.
   Eve and Adam were lots like me and you—
   They did what God their Father told them
   not to do.

3. But God sent Jesus to be our special Friend;
   God sent Jesus—His love will never end.
   God sent Jesus to take our sin away.
   God's love makes us so happy, we all shout
   HOORAY!

God So Loved the World He Gave

1. God so loved the world He gave,
   God so loved the world He gave,
   God so loved the world He gave
   His one and only Son.

2. Those who believe in Jesus Christ,
   Those who believe in Jesus Christ,
   Those who believe in Jesus Christ
   Have eternal life.

God's Covenant

1. Moses climbed up to Mt. Sinai;
   God had said, "Come, meet with Me.
   Listen then and tell My people
   I have set them free."

Refrain
   And God said,
   "Like an eagle bears its young
   On its wings, I've carried you.
   You are Mine, My holy people
   And my precious treasure, too."

2. "Other gods will only hurt you;
   Worship Me and Me alone.
   Use My name in pray'r and praises
   Bowing at My throne."
   REFRAIN

3. "Show My care to those around you
   In the things you say and do.
   Live in joy and peace and always
   Let My love shine through."
   REFRAIN

God's Creation

1. On the first day God created light and darkness,
   day and night.
   On the second He created water and the sky;
   On the third day plants and trees, each one
   having fruit with seed.
   On the fourth day sun for light, moon and stars
   to shine at night.

2. On the fifth day God created creatures of the
   sea and sky,
   Fish for swimming in the water, birds with wings
   to fly.
   On the sixth day God created living creatures of
   the land—
   Then the animals and cattle, all were made by
   His command.

3. God created men and women on the sixth day
   of His plan.
   They were formed in God's own image, made to
   rule the land.
   Though they sinned, God sent a Savior—
   Jesus Christ His only Son.
   By His death and resurrection He gives life to
   ev'ryone.

God's Plan

1. We are God's creation,
   the family of man.
   God showed how much He loves us
   back when the world began.
   When Eve and Adam disobeyed,
   God did not turn away.
   He said He'd send a Savior
   to wash their sins away.

2. God is our Redeemer,
   He's our Creator, too.
   He had a special plan for us
   back when the world was new.
   For we are just like Adam was;
   sometimes we disobey.
   But in Christ Jesus we now know
   our sins are washed away.

Hallelujah! Praise Ye the Lord!

Hallelu! Hallelu! Hallelu! Hallelujah!
Praise ye the Lord!
Hallelu! Hallelu! Hallelu! Hallelujah!
Praise ye the Lord!
Praise ye the Lord! Hallelujah!
Praise ye the Lord! Hallelujah!
Praise ye the Lord! Hallelujah!
Praise ye the Lord!

Have No Fear, Little Flock

1. Have no fear, little flock;
   Have no fear, little flock,
   For the Father has chosen
   To give you the Kingdom;
   Have no fear, little flock!

2. Have good cheer, little flock;
   Have good cheer, little flock,
   For the Father will keep you
   In His love forever;
   Have good cheer, little flock!

3. Praise the Lord high above;
   Praise the Lord high above,
   For He stoops down to heal you,
   Uplift and restore you;
   Praise the Lord high above!

4. Thankful hearts raise to God;
   Thankful hearts raise to God,
   For He stays close beside you,
   In all things works with you;
   Thankful hearts raise to God!

He Is Risen

1. He is risen—(*Yes, indeed!*)
   He is risen—(*Yes, indeed!*)
   Our Lord Jesus is alive! He is not dead.

2. He is with us, He is with us.
   Our Lord Jesus is alive! He is not dead.

3. He will hear us—(*Yes, indeed!*)
   He will hear us—(*Yes, indeed!*)
   Our Lord Jesus is alive, just as He said.

4. He forgives us, He forgives us.
   Our Lord Jesus is alive, just as He said.

Heaven Is a Wonderful Place

Heaven is a wonderful place,
filled with glory and grace.
I wanna see my Savior's face.
Heaven is a wonderful place
(*I wanna go there!*)

He's Alive

1. Why are you weeping? Please don't cry!
   God sent His only Son to die.
   He had a plan, Christ is the way
   For us to live with Him someday.
   He's alive!
   He's alive!
   He is alive!

2. Go tell the others, tell them now
   The stone's been moved, you don't know how.
   The tomb is empty, He's not there,
   And you have very good news to share.
   He's alive!
   He's alive!
   He is alive!

3. Mary, Peter, James and John,
   Jesus our Brother now lives on.
   He has proven His Word true
   And we will live forever, too.
   He's alive!
   He's alive!
   He is alive!

Hosanna, Hallelujah

Refrain

Hosanna, hallelujah!
Sing we loud and clear.
Hosanna, hallelujah! Jesus Christ is near.
With ancient psalms and new-grown palms
Praise Him on His way. Hosanna, hallelujah!
Christ, our Lord, is here.

1. This day in spring the streets will ring with
   voices sweet and lyrical
   To greet our Lord, the One adored,
   His very life a miracle.
   REFRAIN

2. King David's Son now rides upon a mule, of
   beasts the lowliest;
   Amidst the throng it bears along
   of all mankind the holiest.
   REFRAIN

3. How very odd the Son of God must do things
   that would weary us.
   God will amaze; He works in ways
   that we all find mysterious.
   REFRAIN

I Love to Tell the Story

1. I love to tell the story of how, from heaven above
   Our Lord and Savior Jesus was sent to show God's love
   To ev'ry sinful creature upon this earthly place,
   How Christ, the gift from heaven, is God's great gift of grace.

Refrain
I love to tell the story;
'Twill be my theme in glory
to tell the old, old story
Of Jesus and His love.

2. I love to tell the story of how the people came
   To see Him feed the hungry, to see Him cure the lame;
   For Jesus shows compassion to those in storm and strife,
   And offers all His children His gift—eternal life.
   REFRAIN

3. I love to tell the story, although it's sad to tell,
   Of how our Lord and Master faced pain and death and hell.
   Dear Jesus, whipped and bleeding, was hung upon the tree
   And died on that Good Friday to save both you and me.
   REFRAIN

4. I love to tell the story of how our Lord and Friend
   Rose up on Easter morning and reigns in highest heav'n.
   The love of God the Father, the Spirit, and the Son
   Has given us salvation, the free gift Jesus won.
   REFRAIN

I Will Sing unto the Lord

I will sing unto the Lord, for
He has triumphed gloriously,
the horse and rider thrown into the sea.
(*Repeat)*
The Lord, my God, my strength, was tested so;
now He is my victory. *(Repeat)*
The Lord is God, and I will praise Him,
my father's God, and I will exalt Him!
The Lord is God, and I will praise Him,
my father's God, and I will exalt Him!

In God We Believe

1. In God we believe: the Creator whose pow'r
In mercy has brought us for worship this hour.
He graciously grants us our years and our days
And blesses with kindness our work and our
ways.

2. In Jesus, the Savior, our hope is secured.
True God and true man once the cross He
endured
To grant our lives wholeness, forgiveness of sin.
With hearts freed from guilt, we know true
peace within.

3. God's Spirit at work in our lives we confess;
With power and truth, the church now He does
bless.
As saints, God's forgiven, one day we shall then
Be living in glory forever. Amen.

Isaiah 40:31

Those who hope in the Lord will renew their
strength.
They will soar on wings like eagles.
They will run and not grow weary.
They will walk and not be faint.
Those who hope in the Lord.

Jesus in the Morning

1. Jesus, Jesus, Jesus in the morning,
   Jesus at the noontime,
   Jesus, Jesus, Jesus when the sun goes down.

2. Love Him, Love Him, Love Him in the morning,
   Love Him at the noontime,
   Love Him, Love Him, Love Him when the sun goes down.

3. Serve Him, Serve Him, Serve Him in the morning,
   Serve Him at the noontime,
   Serve Him, Serve Him, Serve Him when the sun goes down.

4. Thank Him, Thank Him, Thank Him in the morning,
   Thank Him at the noontime,
   Thank Him, Thank Him, Thank Him when the sun goes down.

5. Praise Him, Praise Him, Praise Him in the morning,
   Praise Him at the noontime,
   Praise Him, Praise Him, Praise Him when the sun goes down.

Jesus Loves the Little Ones

1. Jesus loves the little ones like me, me, me.
   Jesus loves the little ones like me, me, me.
   Little ones like me sat upon His knee.
   Jesus loves the little ones like me, me, me.

2. Jesus loves the little ones like you, you, you.
   Jesus loves the little ones like you, you, you.
   Little ones like you, Jesus loves you, too.
   Jesus loves the little ones like you, you, you.

Joyful, Joyful We Adore Thee

1. Joyful, joyful we adore Thee,
   God of glory, Lord of love!
   Hearts unfold like flow'rs before Thee,
   Praising Thee, their sun above.
   Melt the clouds of sin and sadness,
   Drive the gloom of doubt away.
   Giver of immortal gladness,
   Fill us with the light of day.

2. All Thy works with joy surround Thee,
   Earth and heav'n reflect Thy rays,
   Stars and angels sing around Thee,
   Center of unbroken praise.
   Field and forest, vale and mountain,
   Flow'ry meadow, flashing sea,
   Chanting bird, and flowing fountain
   Call us to rejoice in Thee.

3. Thou art giving and forgiving,
   Ever blessing, ever blest,
   Wellspring of the joy of living,
   Ocean-depth of happy rest!
   Thou our Father, Christ our brother,
   All who live in love are Thine;
   Teach us how to love each other,
   Lift us to the joy divine!

Kids of the Kingdom

1. Kids of the kingdom, that's what we are:
   kids of the kingdom, that's what we are.
   We love Jesus, we love the Lord.
   We love Jesus, we love the lord.

2. My name is ____________. I love the Lord.
   My name is ____________. I love the Lord.
   They love Jesus, they love the Lord.
   They love Jesus, they love the Lord.

3. Kids of the kingdom, that's what we are:
   kids of the kingdom, that's what we are.
   We love Jesus, we love the Lord.
   We love Jesus, we love the Lord.

4. Praise to the Father, praise to the Son,
   praise to the Spirit, the Three in One.
   We love Jesus, we love the Lord.
   We love Jesus, we love the Lord.

Life Is Ours, a Gift from Jesus

1. Life is ours, a gift from Jesus.
   Life that blesses, life that frees us.
   Children of the Father's pleasure.
   We now share our Savior's treasure.

2. Once in sorrow He was crying.
   On a cross our Lord was dying.
   Why should He, God's glory sharing,
   Die for us, God's love not sparing?

3. Oh, the answer is the treasure!
   It brings joy beyond all measure.
   Jesus died new life to nourish.
   Jesus lives that life might flourish.

4. Not a day nor year shall pass us
   When His love will not caress us.
   We shall live our lives believing
   That His life we are receiving.

5. So then join in holy laughter
   Both here now and then hereafter.
   Trust the promise! Hear the sending!
   Sing a song of life unending!

Lord's Prayer

Our Father who art in heaven,
  hallowed be Thy name,
Thy kingdom come, Thy will be done
  on earth as it is in heaven.
Give us this day our daily bread;
and forgive us our trespasses
  as we forgive those who trespass against us;
and lead us not into temptation,
  but deliver us from evil.
For Thine is the kingdom and the pow'r
  and the glory forever and ever.
Amen. Amen. Amen.

Making Melody in My Heart

Making melody in my heart,
Making melody in my heart,
Making melody in my heart
Unto the King of kings!
Worship and adore Him!
Worship and adore Him!
Making melody in my heart
Unto the King of kings!

Oh, He's King of Kings

Refrain

Oh, He's King of kings,
Oh, He's Lord of lords!
Jesus Christ, the First and Last,
No man works like Him.

1. I know that my Redeemer lives,
No man works like Him,
And by His love sweet blessings gives,
No man works like Him.
REFRAIN

2. Victorious at God's right hand,
No man works like Him,
He calls His saints from ev'ry land,
No man works like Him.
REFRAIN

Our Hearts Are Overflowing

Our hearts are overflowing, Lord, with thankfulness.
Our hearts are overflowing, Lord, with thankfulness.
We give thanks for the day, thanks for the food, thanks for these friends we love.
Our hearts are overflowing, Lord, with thankfulness.
We give thanks for our faith, thanks for our joy, thanks for Your precious love.
Our hearts are overflowing, Lord, with thankfulness.

Praise Him, Praise Him

1. Praise Him, praise Him, all you little children;
   God is love, God is love.
   Praise Him, praise Him, all you little children;
   God is love, God is love.

2. Love Him, love Him, all you little children;
   God is love, God is love.
   Love Him, love Him, all you little children;
   God is love, God is love.

3. Thank Him, thank Him, all you little children;
   God is love, God is love.
   Thank Him, thank Him, all you little children;
   God is love, God is love.

4. Serve Him, serve Him, all you little children;
   God is love, God is love.
   Serve Him, serve Him, all you little children;
   God is love, God is love.

Rejoice! Rejoice!

Rejoice! Rejoice!
All be glad! All be glad!
Rejoice! Rejoice!
Our Savior reigns!

Seek Ye First

1. Seek ye first the Kingdom of God,
   And His righteousness.
   And all these things shall be added unto you!
   Allelu, alleluia!

2. Ask and it shall be giv'n unto you,
   Seek and ye shall find,
   Knock and the door shall be opened unto you,
   Allelu, alleluia!

3. Man does not live by bread alone,
   But by ev'ry word
   That proceeds from the mouth of the Lord,
   Allelu, alleluia!

Shalom, My Friends

Shalom, my friends!
Shalom, my friends!
Shalom! Shalom!
God's peace be with you!
God's peace be with you!
Shalom! Shalom!

Silver and Gold

1. Silver and gold have I none,
   But such as I have give I thee;
   In the name of Jesus Christ of Nazareth,
   rise up and walk!

Refrain

He went walking and leaping and praising God,
walking and leaping and praising God.
In the name of Jesus Christ of Nazareth,
rise up and walk.

2. Fear and hate have I none,
   Because of Jesus Christ.
   He helped the blind to see
   So ev'ryone stand up and praise.
   REFRAIN

3. Power and strength have I none,
   But Jesus gave me life
   So I can be happy and glad,
   Because He loves me so.
   REFRAIN

So Go!

God makes all kinds of people ev'rywhere.
He makes each of us special,
    doesn't make a single pair.
He loves us as we are
    and wants us to believe
Jesus took away our sins and set us free!

So Go (*Go!*) Tell! (*Tell!*) friends and neighbors,
    too.
God's love for us is so amazing,
    wonderful, and true.
His Son, our Savior Jesus
    died and rose so we could be
Made a special part of His family.
So Go! (*repeat st. 2*)

The Best Book of All

The best book of all is the Bible;
It tells about Jesus, God's Son.
It tells of the good home in heaven;
It tells that God loves every one.

The King's Kids Are Prayin'

Refrain

The King's kids are prayin' to Jesus, our King,
Oh, the King's kids are prayin' for everything!
We're gonna ASK! SEEK! KNOCK! and we're gonna sing,
'Cause we're talkin' with our Savior.
He's Jesus, our King!

1. We pray and say "Thank You," oh, every day,
We talk to our Father, He hears when we pray.
We tell Him our sins, and He takes them away.
We have His forgiveness. Let's shout, "Hooray!"
REFRAIN

2. We thank You, Lord Jesus, for loving us so!
We're prayin' for others wherever we go.
We listen to You, and we hear what You say.
We're trustin' in You, Lord. Show us the way.
Spoken: The King's kids are prayin'!
The King's kids are prayin'!
Prayin' to Jesus!
Sung: The King's kids are prayin' to Jesus, our King!
Spoken: Jesus, our King!

There Were Twelve Disciples

There were twelve disciples
Jesus called to help Him:
Simon Peter, Andrew, James, his brother
John;
Philip, Thomas, Matthew, James, the son of
Alpheus;
Thaddeus, Simon, Judas, and Bartholomew.
He has called us, too;
He has called us, too.
We are His disciples;
I am one, and you.
He has called us, too;
He has called us, too.
We are His disciples;
We His work must do.

We Pray for Each Other

1. We pray for each other, For sister and brother,
   For father and mother; Dear God, bless us all.

2. We pray for the sick ones, The strong and the weak ones,
   The brave and the meek ones; Dear God, bless us all.

3. We ask this through Jesus, Our Savior, who loves us
   And from our sin frees us. Dear God, bless us all.

We'll Give All the Glory to Jesus

We'll give all the glory to Jesus
and tell of His love,
and tell of His love.
We'll give all the glory to Jesus
and tell of His wonderful love.

Yes

And God said

Refrain

Yes to you! He said Yes to me
When the Baptism water flowed freely.
In the name of the Father, the Spirit, the Son,
Our journey of faith had begun.
And God said
Yes to you! He said Yes to me
When the Baptism water flowed freely.
In the name of the Father, the Spirit, the Son,
Our journey of faith had begun.

1. Oh, it's amazing grace indeed
That would save someone like me:
Saved by grace so amazingly free.
Oh, it's an awesome, lovely sound,
It's the sweetest sound around;
It's the Good News for you and for me.
That God said
REFRAIN

2. But there's the devil on the prowl
Seeking whom he may devour
Off'ring all kinds of fortune and fame.
But when the devil seeks his due
For the things he's offered you,
Just say, "No! I don't play Satan's game!"
And God said
REFRAIN

3. Oh, each and ev'ry day is great
It's a day to celebrate
What the Lord, in His mercy, has done.
Whatever any day shall bring
Live each day for Christ the King!
Live each day as a victory won!
And God said
REFRAIN

You Will Be My Witness

You will be My witness to the world,

You will tell them how I love them,
tell them all I've done.
You will be My witness to the world,
In Jerusalem, Judea, Samaria, and all the
earth.
Wait for the gift from our Father you have
heard Me speak of.
You will be given power by the Holy Spirit.
You will be My witness to the world,
You will tell them how I love them,
tell them all I've done.
You will be My witness to the world,
In Jerusalem, Judea, Samaria and all the
earth.